EVEN *the* DEMONS BELIEVE

TIMOTHY WILLIAMS

WINEPRESS **WP** PUBLISHING

First edition printed January 2001
Second edition printed July 2001
Third edition printed January 2003

Printed in Hong Kong by YTL.

Published by WinePress Publishing,
PO Box 428, Enumclaw, WA 98022.

ISBN 1-57921-355-3
Library of Congress Catalog Card Number: 00-111854

Cover design by His Workmanship

Dedicated to all who love God enough to reject cheap grace.

Again, the kingdom of heaven is like a merchant look-ing for fine pearls. When he found one of great value, he went away and sold everything he had and bought it. (Matthew 13:45–46)

Contents

FOREWORD

As you open this book, my wife and I would like to share our experiences in both extremes of Christianity, from cheap grace to legalistic. I personally grew up in the charismatic church and now, looking back, I am amazed at the things I believed. How could I look at Jesus' life and think it was so easy to follow Him? Most Sunday messages consisted of stories, jokes, or experiences of the pastor, yet held no power. It was like going to children's church for adults. At the conclusion of every sermon, and after the moral of the story was revealed, everyone bowed their heads. The Pastor would then ask if anyone wanted to be saved or felt a tugging at their hearts to raise their hands, repeat a prayer, and instantly receive salvation. I did that. I can't count how many times I raised my hand, yet it never caused my heart to change. No one ever told me how to count the cost of following Christ. I could keep sinning and still be covered by God's "grace," but never change. I didn't know what it meant to be a disciple and certainly no one ever warned me of the cost. My wife tells a different story.

———————————

Growing up I (Jessica) had very little experience with church. When Greg and I met, neither of us walked with the Lord. Then right before we married, I started searching for a church. A friend told me of a small non-denominational church that seemed to preach the truth. Greg and I began to attend there regularly. Since my life was ridden with sin, I felt convicted every time I heard a sermon. At this church, I saw a lot of things in me that needed to change and was taught that if the Bible says it, you do it. After time, however, my heart started to feel heavier and heavier as if I was dying a very slow death. I found it impossible to do what the scriptures and sermons said. This confused me deeply. My relationships with people at church grew colder and colder. I began to cry out to God to show me what I was doing wrong. I wanted to change and obey Him, but my Christianity was powerless. The church leaders concluded that I struggled because I hadn't gone up to the altar and asked Jesus into my heart, even though they had baptized me. The more I questioned and asked for guidance, the more they placed legalistic rules on me. Eventually, they asked me to leave and not come back. Finally, Greg and I saw the deception of the church's controlling rules and left.

———————————

Neither Jessica or myself (Greg) wanted to run from God, but with my liberal past and now this experience, we grew more and more confused. The passage about walking the narrow road plagued Jessica, but we had no idea where to find it. At the end of our rope, the Lord revealed to us a Christianity with power, the message of the cross.

One day Jessica caught the tale end of a radio program and checked the website given by the author of this book. The teaching sounded much like what we had just left, yet we sensed something different. We felt God's love and strength in the message. It seemed to balance receiving God's grace with denying ourselves. This message gave us hope because we learned that we could change by God's power.

Coming from the "we are free to do whatever and covered by the blood" to the "if the Bible says it, do it" extremes, we felt hungry and unsatisfied. On hearing the message of the cross we became full of joy, yet at the same time overwhelmed with the power and love of God. My wife and I had no idea the life changing experience that God would bring. No longer did we walk on a wide path leading to cheap, easy grace. We discovered that God's grace teaches us to say "No" to sin and pride. Jessica found that she could be accepted by God and walk and change by the power of the Spirit. The message of the cross is no easy believism, nor is it harsh legalism.

While reading this you might say, "This can't be right" or maybe you will fall on your face before God as we did. Please do not take counting the cost lightly. The cross has brought us extreme joy and at the same time overwhelming helplessness, knowing that we can do nothing without Jesus, which is exactly where God wants us to be.

In some ways, this message felt harder than the one before, because at the cross our deepest sins are revealed. God's love seems unbearable at times because for our benefit He disciplines us. At the cross, however, Jessica and I began to work out our own salvation with fear and trembling. There we have found joy in our marriage and a relationship with the Lord that we never experienced before. It's not enough to walk by the rules laid down by God in the Bible—true salvation comes by doing it solely by His power. And it's not enough to quickly accept His grace and say we believe in God—because even the demons believe.

Greg & Jessica Gambill

CHAPTER 1

Which Way to Salvation?

This is what the Lord says: "Stand at the crossroads and look; ask for the ancient paths, ask where the good way is, and walk in it, and you will find rest for your souls . . ." (Jeremiah 6:16)

Every church has their method for getting to heaven, so how can a person know the correct path? With all the different beliefs and opinions about what it means to be a Christian, no wonder so many people feel thoroughly confused.[1] In fact, many have given up the search for God altogether because the task to discover the truth seems too overwhelming. Additionally, many today falsely think that opinion equals belief, and if we think something sincerely enough, God will accept us. To further compound the problem, multitudes of hypocritical "Christians" claim they know God. All of these things and more frustrate those with an honest search for God.

To find the answers, we need to follow Jeremiah's direction: "Ask for the ancient paths, ask where the good way is" and then "walk in it." Through these God-given words we will find "rest for" our "souls."

In Luke 7:48 Jesus told a woman, "Your sins are forgiven." God forgave every wrong thing in her actions and thoughts. Those words are the sweetest words a man or woman can ever hear.

God's forgiveness should set us free and light our hearts aflame with an undying love for Him.[2] In order to hear those words, we must first consider what it means to be a Christian. Otherwise, we place ourselves in danger of being "denounced" by the very God who touches our lives with love and power.[3] As the following Scripture demonstrates, Jesus disowned those whom God had touched in a powerful way because they would not "repent." With this in mind, let us look at what it really means to be a Christian, how one becomes a Christian, and the requirements to keep from being "denounce[d]" by God. In short, let us see the truth according to Jesus.

> Then Jesus began to denounce the cities in which most of his miracles had been performed, because they did not repent. (Matthew 11:20)

When Jesus walked on the earth, He made Christians in a very odd fashion. Jesus won souls, as we shall see, in a manner that may surprise most.[4] This book examines how someone becomes a Christian according to Jesus.

Most individuals, who consider themselves Christians, have responded to God's love in a way that would not receive Jesus' approval. As Paul stated in the book of Romans, they did not "submit" to God's way of salvation and instead "sought to establish their own."

Since they did not know the righteousness that comes from God and sought to establish their own, they did not submit to God's righteousness. (Romans 10:3)

Every church and denomination has their methods for saving individuals. Each has "established their own" way of salvation. But God declared long ago that only "one" way leads to heaven.

. . . one Lord, one faith, one baptism . . . (Ephesians 4:5)

Each man must make a decision to either submit to God's righteousness or embrace man's religious ways. God's righteousness grows eternally, but the peace and security of man offers only empty hope.

In the church today, we have established many different ways to become a Christian. People can come forward after a sermon, raise their hands, attend classes, speak in tongues, or repeat the words someone tells them to say. The salvation calls, coming forward to accept Jesus, vary from church to church, but which one is of God? Let us go back and look at how Jesus made someone a Christian. We will look at Jesus' salvation call,[5] and if it does not match up to ours, let us repent and "submit to God's righteousness."

Truths to Ponder, Beliefs to Examine

- What opinions do you hold about the way of salvation?

- Why do you hold these opinions? Where did you learn them?

- If you submit to God's righteousness, what might happen to these beliefs?

- Are you ready to examine your beliefs deeper?

CHAPTER 2

Even Demons Believe in God

Most believe in God and the vast majority of the world is religious. Even those who do not believe in God have faith in their belief that there is no God. Those without a specific belief foolishly believe in themselves.[6] Therefore, it is safe to say every man believes in something. Believing comes easy to man, because God has given him this ability.[7] Unfortunately, man has invented many things to believe in. The number of "schemes" man creates in order to satisfy his desires to believe are indeed "many."

This only have I found: God made mankind upright, but men have gone in search of many schemes. (Ecclesiastes 7:29)

Christianity is no exception. The Christian church searched out and created many different "schemes" to get to Jesus. Those "schemes" range from just asking Jesus into your heart, speaking in tongues, signing the back of a Bible, saying the Rosary, to being water baptized. Let us return to the path Jesus set down and accept His instructions for belief in God.

"If anyone comes to me . . ." (Luke 14:26)

"If anyone comes to" Jesus for salvation, he must understand specific things right up front. The cost must be counted before anyone declares themselves a Christian. Before a man or woman can claim the saving power of Jesus, they must count the cost demanded for salvation.

To merely believe and confess with your mouth that Jesus is Lord without matching action creates demonic faith that perverts the following Scripture.

> For it is with your heart that you believe and are justified, and it is with your mouth that you confess and are saved. (Romans 10:10)

After all, don't the demons meet the requirements preached in most churches? Do not demons believe God exists? Do not demons even confess that Jesus is the Holy One of God?[8] Of course they do. Therefore to quote only Romans 10:10 while ignoring the rest of God's Word makes one's faith equal to that of demons.

> You believe that there is one God. Good! Even the demons believe that—and shudder. (James 2:19)

You believe in God. Great, even the demons, who will be tortured in hell, believe in God. Your opinion about God means nothing, just as the demons' beliefs about God do not keep them from being demonic. In fact, the difference between men and demons is that demons at least "shudder." They know enough to fear God and by the time the majority of people find out that their beliefs are lifeless, they too will "shudder." Demons feel terrified as to what will happen to them and we should be too, unless we repent. Demons, as well as all who have not repented as God commands, will "shout[ed] at the top" of their "voices" pleading with God not to "torture" them.

> He shouted at the top of his voice, "What do you want with me, Jesus, Son of the Most High God? Swear to God that you won't torture me!" (Mark 5:7)

God has an "appointed time" to literally "torture" those with demonic faith based on selfish motives and sin.

> "What do you want with us, Son of God?" they shouted. "Have you come here to torture us before the appointed time?" (Matthew 8:29)

You can hear their voices and almost feel their fear of being tortured by God.[9] We do well to take a hard honest look at what we call faith in God.[10] Most confuse faith in God with their "opinion" about spiritual matters. Others think of faith as simply declaring that they have asked God to come into their life. First, only a "fool delights" in his opinions about God. So the next time you find yourself in a group, school, or Sunday school class where everyone gives their opinions about God, feel free to quote the following Scripture.

A fool finds no pleasure in understanding but delights in airing his own opinions. (Proverbs 18:2)

Secondly, most have come to God by simply asking Him into their lives. Their belief is merely opinion expressed with conviction. In other words, they believe they have God because they asked Him to come into their life. This corruption of Romans 10:10 takes away the saltiness of Jesus' salvation message.

Demons love it when people preach Romans 10:10 to the exclusion of the rest of Scripture, for this is what made them demons. They rejected God's perfect plan for them in favor of their own opinions, wants, and desires. Satan told Eve this same old lie when he cast doubt on what God said. Satan still performs the same old trick of asking, "Did God really say this is the way to be saved?"[11]

Many people become increasingly demonic in the name of Jesus. They think the sole requirement is to just "believe" in God. Without obedience or "action," however, a person cannot be saved. Remember, the demons believe in God but have no good action and thus their faith cannot save them.

In short, godly faith equals action, and obedience with the Holy Spirit expresses honest faith.[12] On the other hand, faith without God's "action" is merely man's opinions worked out for his own selfish ends.

In the same way, faith by itself, if it is not accompanied by action, is dead. (James 2:17)

Truths to Ponder, Beliefs to Examine

- What is wrong with the "just believe and you're saved" teaching?

- What cost did you pay to become a Christian?

- In what ways did you discover the price higher than you thought?

CHAPTER 3

Large Crowds Traveling
with Jesus

Large crowds" attend church today and "large crowds" come to hear preachers talk about Jesus. "Large crowds" of people buy books, listen to sermon tapes, and talk about Bible issues. Many individuals attend Bible College and seminary to study about God. There are "large crowds" "traveling" with Jesus and yet not a single one of them will go to heaven. Mere "travelers" will burn in hell forever.

Large crowds were traveling . . . (Luke 14:25)

We must understand the difference between a true Christian and a traveler following Jesus. A traveler comes along for the ride, enjoying the free food, miracles, and blessings of Jesus, yet they reject His way of salvation. They remain belly believers, and their faith always strives to get something from God.

> Their destiny is destruction, their god is their stomach, and their glory is in their shame. Their mind is on earthly things. (Philippians 3:19)

Travelers who follow Jesus to get something from Him should take warning. Jesus seeks to tell us "the truth" about ourselves; that we follow Him only because He will meet our selfish needs. Many want to eat "the loaves" and have their "fill" of peace, prosperity, happiness, blessings, and hope but refuse to fall in love with Him.

> Jesus answered, "I tell you the truth, you are looking for me, not because you saw miraculous signs but because you ate the loaves and had your fill." (John 6:26)

People prove their belly belief true when they reject the cross, God's way of saving a man. They follow Jesus, but have little interest in the cross, except that Jesus died for them. The church today contains multitudes of "travelers." Many consider themselves strong Christians, but they are mere travelers, not true disciples of Jesus. Jesus turned to these "large crowds" of travelers and spoke of the seriousness of calling oneself a Christian.

> Large crowds were traveling with Jesus, and turning to them he said: . . . (Luke 14:25)

The truth is, Jesus wasn't trying to make anyone a Christian; rather, Jesus came and died to make disciples. We will see the importance of this later on. For now, let us listen to Jesus as He speaks of God's salvation call or God's way of saving individuals. Man wants to entertain and make it easy to accept Jesus, while God tests and drives away all unworthy of eternal life.[13] Jesus' ways are for "anyone" who desires salvation. Jesus is emphatic about this.

If anyone comes . . . (Luke 14:26)

And anyone . . . (Luke 14:27)

Jesus spent over three years getting people ready for Peter's sermon at Pentecost. We, however, declare individuals to be Christians without ever preparing them. The church's interest in numbers motivates leaders to declare a new birth before conception has barely taken place. Paul compares Christ coming into a person's life to that of the process of childbirth,[14] but in our fleshly zeal we skip the suffering of pregnancy and delivery in order to justify our own sin. Wouldn't you think it strange for a husband to shout, "Come see my baby" if his wife was only one month along?

God spent thousands of years getting things ready for Jesus to come and preach the good news. Why then do we think someone is saved when we have to teach them the words to say in their own salvation prayer?

Jesus tested and tried people; He made them think, ponder, and become frustrated concerning the things of God in order to test their hunger for God.[15]

Like spoiled children whose parents anticipate and fill their every possible desire, we make salvation simple. We give people all the answers and make it easy for them to accept our version of Christianity, but we are not saving their souls.

As a result, we label mere travelers following Jesus as saved Christians, when nothing could be further from the truth. In our day the message of counting the cost is met with outright hostility because we have so cheapened the grace of God. What will you do? Will you change from a "traveler" to becoming a "disciple?"

Truths to Ponder, Beliefs to Examine

- Who do you think the "large crowds" are today? Why do they follow Jesus?

- Explain the difference between a true follower and a traveler with Jesus.

- In what aspects of your life do you think you merely travel with Jesus? List some things you could do to become a follower.

CHAPTER 4

Christian or Disciple?

The man who loves his life will lose it, while the man who hates his life in this world will keep it for eternal life. (John 12:25)

Jesus hated His life while He walked on this earth. He hated His life and carried His cross. The message of hating one's life is the good news[16] Jesus preached and lived. Only this message saves a man from hell and honestly blesses his life. Without this hatred Jesus says no one will gain "eternal life."

Many think that Jesus' teaching about hating is not for young believers or for those considering becoming a Christian. They wrongly believe that somehow presenting this tough message up front will only scare people away. But it was not so with Jesus, for He was always blunt about the cross. He remained upfront and bold about the requirements of becoming a Christian. Jesus never said the Christian life would be easy.[17]

Jesus never put out a simple salvation call asking individuals to come forward if they wanted to be saved. Jesus never told crowds to raise their hands and just ask Him into their heart. Scripture never records anyone just asking Jesus into their heart by reciting a canned "believer's prayer." In fact, you will not find most modern methods of receiving salvation in the Bible. More specifically, today's methods of coming to the Lord hardly shadow what Jesus had in mind.

In the first place, Jesus did not come to make Christians, but disciples. This is an important distinction, mainly because when someone refers to themselves as a Christian they consider it a done deal. But Jesus looked at it differently. He sought to make disciples, and a disciple is someone in the act of continually learning from God. Even Jesus "learned obedience from what he suffered." Jesus, as the Son of Man, was the perfect disciple in whose steps we must follow.[18]

Although he was a son, he learned obedience from what he suffered. (Hebrews 5:8)

Becoming a disciple demands a degree of humility and teachability that being a Christian does not require. A Christian sounds like a finished deal. Think of a student in medical school learning what will make him a doctor. Not until graduation day can he call himself a doctor. So too, we will not really be Christians, people fully made in the image of Jesus, until we graduate and see Him "face to face."[19]

Even in the world, anyone desiring to become a physician must consider the cost to see if they are willing to pay the price to finish school. Just like the medical profession, many drop out and fall away from Jesus.[20]

Worldly non-believers first called disciples of Jesus "Christians."[21] The pagan world used this derogatory term while true believers of Jesus always referred to themselves as "disciples."[22]

The word "disciple" means a student, learner, or pupil. A disciple is in the process of being saved and waits for God's "coming of salvation," "revealed in the last time."[23]

> . . . who through faith are shielded by God's power until the coming of the salvation that is ready to be revealed in the last time. (1 Peter 1:5)

Jesus' salvation call speaks only of making "disciples." In the great commission of Matthew 28:19, Jesus does not say go make Christians; He bids us instead to go make "disciples." All through Luke 14:25–35, Jesus declares that if we do not agree to these things we cannot be a disciple. Only a disciple receives salvation.

> . . . he cannot be my disciple. (Luke 14:26)

> . . . cannot be my disciple. (Luke 14:27)

> . . . cannot be my disciple. (Luke 14:33)

So Jesus poses the questions, "Are you willing to become a disciple? Are you willing to pay the price to be disciplined and become a disciple to the very end of your life?" Before you say "Yes," Jesus wants you to "sit down" and think about your decision.

Truths to Ponder, Beliefs to Examine

- Jesus "learned" obedience to God through suffering. What kinds of suffering do you think God puts a disciple through?

- Why do we need to continually learn from God? What might happen if we stopped learning?

- Sit down and ask yourself, "Am I willing to suffer to become a disciple?"

First Sit Down

Will he not first sit down . . . ~Jesus

Jesus did not say, "Come on down to the front of the church and accept Me as your personal Lord and Savior." Jesus did not say, "Come get your blessing." Nor did Jesus apply rules to your life in order to receive salvation from hell. Jesus said that anyone even remotely thinking about becoming a Christian must first "sit down and estimate the cost."

He said, "sit down" and consider very carefully what it means to follow Him. Without emotional fanfare, Jesus calls all who desire His salvation to "sit down" and do some very sober thinking. Jesus never worked the crowds in order to gain followers, rather He always called for them to quietly "sit down" and "estimate" the cost of being saved. "Suppose one of you wants to build a tower . . ." and just "suppose one of you wants to" be a disciple . . . then "sit down."

> Suppose one of you wants to build a tower. Will he not first sit down and estimate the cost to see if he has enough money to complete it? For if he lays the foundation and is not able to finish it, everyone who sees it will ridicule him, saying, "This fellow began to build and was not able to finish." (Luke 14:28–30)

Many did not count the cost of laying a "foundation" only later to quit. Therefore do not take lightly Jesus' words about counting the cost. If those who did count the cost later decided it was not worth finishing the tower, then how much more should you, with sober thought, consider what it will cost you? Sad to say, many are "ridicule[d]" today because they counted the cost but later became unwilling to pay the price for full redemption from sin. Indeed, the next passage reveals that many of Jesus' "disciples," not mere travelers, left because the crucified life became too much for them.

> From this time many of his disciples turned back and no longer followed him. (John 6:66)

Many might think this all sounds like salvation by works and an attempt to earn God's salvation. But truthfully, Jesus declared that in order to receive God's free mercy, we must let go of all. Those who whine that this is salvation by works miss the whole point. Disciples simply respond to God's mercy everyday. Like "rain" that falls on good soil, it produces a "useful crop."[24] If the soil becomes hard, nothing of value can grow.[25] If a man hardens his heart, cutting off the power of grace, he will forfeit eternal life.[26] A disciple simply says "Yes" to the grace of God every day. This is the test, to say "Yes" to God at all times out of love for Him. If we do that, God can keep us from falling. God will never, however, force a man to be saved if he is unwilling to allow grace to flow through him.[27] If we refuse the grace that crucifies self, then we will be cut off, "thrown away," and eventually "burned" in hell.[28]

No man who truly wants to be rid of the sins in his life considers this a cost at all. "In his joy" the true disciple sells "all" to buy the "treasure" of God's grace and mercy. In short, it only sounds hard and legalistic to the hard-hearted. For only the hard-hearted and hard-headed refuse to give up all in exchange for a "treasure."

> The kingdom of heaven is like treasure hidden in a field. When a man found it, he hid it again, and then in his joy went and sold all he had and bought that field. (Matthew 13:44)

The treasure of Jesus is "hidden," God doesn't give knowledge about the message of the cross to everyone. It is too valuable and powerful for God to let the wicked trample upon it. Many religious churchgoers never find this treasure. While many who do find it never go back to it because they didn't "sit down" and think about the matter between themselves and God. They lose the treasure through confusion.

Once a man finds this treasure, he conceals it or keeps it to himself. Indeed, he hides it again, so that others are not aware of why he is selling everything. He becomes very quiet, contemplating alone what he has found between himself and God.[29] Unlike so many who go out to find opinion after opinion about what others think about Jesus, this man realizes the value and ponders it between himself and God. Those with bad hearts go from person to person, book to book exposing the treasure to the evaluation of men. They take before sinful man that which the Holy Spirit has opened their eyes to. They treat the treasure of grace as if it were a trinket found in the sand on a beach. How sad to watch so many, as God points them to the treasure, go out and become thoroughly confused as to whether Jesus, or the message of the cross, really is of God. Finally in their confusion they give up and refuse to dig up again the treasure they found earlier. The treasure became tarnished by man's hands, voices, commentaries, and watering down the gospel. Those who will not "sit down," with the treasure of God hidden again, will never find eternal life. It is "good" for a man or woman, when they discover the message of the cross, to "wait quietly for the salvation of the Lord."

> The Lord is good to those whose hope is in him, to the one who seeks him; it is good to wait quietly for the salvation of the Lord. (Lamentations 3:25–26)

Truths to Ponder, Beliefs to Examine

- What would you consider the "treasures" of God?

- In what ways do you find waiting for God difficult?

CHAPTER 6

God's Terms of Peace

Jesus said to the woman, "Your faith has saved you; go in peace." (Luke 7:50)

Go in peace," Jesus told the woman forgiven of sin. The world hungers for peace and countless men and women search to find some tranquility in their lives. This feeling cannot be achieved or found until they find peace with God. God is the only source for lasting peace and when we discover rest with Him we obtain the Peace of all peace. He is the fountain to the rivers of peace that flow through a man's life.[30] Without Him, peace cannot be found.[31] What allowed the woman to hear Jesus' gentle, loving words? What did she have that so many miss?

Jesus came to bring us peace with God, but unfortunately most do not realize that God wars against them.[32] Most falsely believe God is on their side even while their lives remain loaded down with sinfulness. Multitudes of preachers and pastors preach a false message that God has forgiven them without repentance and obedience to God's way of salvation.[33]

While it is true that God loves us, it is also true that right now God prepares to judge the world and to send the vast majority of individuals, whether in the church or outside it, to hell. His just judgment comes and those not at peace with Him will be tortured in hell forever and ever.[34] This is why God tells us to "make every effort" to be saved.[35]

Let's examine how a man comes to peace with a God who is at war with him. What "terms of peace" does Jesus command us to "sit down" and think about?

> Or suppose a king is about to go to war against another king. Will he not first sit down and consider whether he is able with ten thousand men to oppose the one coming against him with twenty thousand? If he is not able, he will send a delegation while the other is still a long way off and will ask for terms of peace. (Luke 14:31–32)

Again Jesus says, "First sit down and consider" what it means to obtain "peace" with God. It is not just a matter of a simple salvation call, speaking in tongues, or asking Jesus in your heart. Indeed, experiencing miracles does not signify that a person is saved.[36] Only those who have sat down, counted the cost, and paid the price, travel the road of salvation.[37]

Since none can pay the price for their sins, we should, while God stays a "long way off" from condemning us, ask for His "terms of peace." Don't ask for your church's terms of peace, nor listen to your opinion about this matter. Get to know God's "terms of peace" and how to accept them, for He leaves no margin for error in this matter.

Join a "delegation" that moves out to meet God on His terms before the judgment day and surrender all. That is, find a church that understands and lives these "terms of peace." And when you find one, join them in their "effort" to be "found spotless, blameless, and at peace with" God.

> So then, dear friends, since you are looking forward to this, make every effort to be found spotless, blameless and at peace with him. (2 Peter 3:14)

Do you really think you can "oppose" God's army? How many foolishly believe their opinion about Scripture will change God's mind? How foolish we are to think that our opinion that discipleship is not required for salvation can prevail against God. Our logical gymnastics will not impede God's judgment from marching forward by a single step. A church's empty definition of grace will not succeed against God's army and survive the battle. It is a war lost before it begins, to try and water down God's way of salvation. Better to fully surrender to God and receive His blessings, than raise one argument that will forfeit paradise.

Truths to Ponder, Beliefs to Examine

- Describe perfect peace.

- What sins in your life do you think God may oppose right now?

- Sit down in prayer and ask God for His terms of peace in your life.

CHAPTER 7

Losing Our Saltiness

Jesus said only the church that understands His salvation call remains "salty." If any church or disciple loses this "salty" quality of God's "terms of peace" it will be "thrown out." It drives one to tears to consider how many different styles of salvation calls will be "thrown out" in the end. The large numbers of individuals supposedly coming to Christ will prove to be the Church's shame,[38] because they rejected Jesus' salvation call and made up one of their own.

> Salt is good, but if it loses its saltiness, how can it be made salty again? It is fit neither for the soil nor for the manure pile; it is thrown out. "He who has ears to hear, let him hear." (Luke 14:34–35)

All those souls being "saved" will be "thrown out" because churches remove counting the cost from their messages. At our own peril, we ignore or change Jesus' salvation call.

The cost of salvation by Jesus is one-hundred-percent. It cost Jesus all to die for our sins, and as a fair exchange, we give Him everything.[39] All preaching to potential converts should involve estimating the cost. If not, the result is a wide gate[40] gospel call that many enter through to their destruction in hell. Jesus flat out declares, without shame, that it will cost a man everything in this world to be saved.

> In the same way, any of you who does not give up everything he has cannot be my disciple. (Luke 14:33)

Again, remember this is the starting point of what it means to be a Christian or a true disciple. This is not the end goal, but the requirement of entering the race of righteousness.[41] Anyone not willing to pay the entrance fee becomes disqualified right from the start. After all, a runner refusing to race "according to the rules" is disqualified from the prize. How many run the race toward God, but not "according to the rules!"[42] In the end, they find themselves disqualified for eternal life.

> Similarly, if anyone competes as an athlete, he does not receive the victor's crown unless he competes according to the rules. (2 Timothy 2:5)

This may sound like someone trying to earn his or her way to heaven. The schemes of man have altered the meaning of true faith in Jesus. When men speak of faith in the church today they falsely believe no matter what people do, if they believe in Jesus, they will go to heaven. That type of faith, without obedience, mocks Jesus' death. Jesus suffered, labored, and died to give us faith that works "obedience" in us.

Through him and for his name's sake, we received grace and apostleship to call people from among all the Gentiles to the *obedience that comes from faith.* (Romans 1:5 emphasis added)

As the Scripture above reveals, Paul preached "grace" that produces "obedience." So true faith in Jesus starts and ends with obedience.[43] This means doing what God commands, in God's power, and in the way God declares things should be done. Without this true faith, our belief equals that of the demons'.

Truths to Ponder, Beliefs to Examine

- Think of the qualities of salt. It gives flavor, it stings if poured on a wound, and it preserves and protects against germs and bacteria. With this in mind, describe a "salty" church.

- Do you think the church today as a whole fits this description? Why or why not?

- List a few of God's rules for running the race of salvation.

CHAPTER 8

Shaking the Salt Shaker

Let us shake the salt shaker just a little and see what a man or woman should consider before calling themselves a disciple of Jesus. The terms of peace, the cost of having true faith in Jesus, are threefold. We each have sinned against the God who is One, but manifested in three in the Trinity, so our repentance is threefold. First, we must hate those around us. Second, we must hate our own life. And third, we must pick up a cross and follow Jesus.

> Large crowds were traveling with Jesus, and turning to them he said: "If anyone comes to me and does not hate his father and mother, his wife and children, his brothers and sisters—yes, even his own life—he cannot be my disciple. And anyone who does not carry his cross and follow me cannot be my disciple." (Luke 14:25–27)

Of course this is not a worldly kind of hate that seeks to do harm to others. Yes, God is love and He desires that we love others.[44] However, we can only love God and others by "hating" and carrying our cross as we follow Jesus.[45] The following list shows just a few things to consider before you make your decision to follow Jesus. Please keep in mind these are only a few things that you should consider long before calling yourself a Christian.

- A complete rejection of all that is sinful.

  Aim for perfection . . . (2 Corinthians 13:11)

- A despising and hating of money.

  No servant can serve two masters. Either he will hate the one and love the other, or he will be devoted to the one and despise the other. You cannot serve both God and Money. (Luke 16:13)

- A total focus only upon the will of God.

  Why, you do not even know what will happen tomorrow. What is your life? You are a mist that appears for a little while and then vanishes. Instead, you ought to say, "If it is the Lord's will, we will live and do this or that." (James 4:14–15)

- A willingness to have all pride put to death.

  The Lord is good to those whose hope is in him, to the one who seeks him; it is good to wait quietly for the salvation of the Lord. It is good for a man to bear the yoke while he is young. Let him sit alone in silence, for the Lord has laid it on him. Let him bury his face in the dust—there may yet be hope. Let him offer his cheek to one who would strike him, and let him be filled with disgrace. (Lamentations 3:25–30)

- An utter rejection of one's opinions and thoughts.

    A fool finds no pleasure in understanding but delights in airing his own opinions. (Proverbs 18:2)

- A new way of doing everything in daily life.

    So from now on we regard no one from a worldly point of view. Though we once regarded Christ in this way, we do so no longer. (2 Corinthians 5:16)

- A hatred of one's time, rest, comfort, fun, and joys.

    The man who loves his life will lose it, while the man who hates his life in this world will keep it for eternal life. (John 12:25)

- Let God transform you into a slave.

    . . . and whoever wants to be first must be slave of all. (Mark 10:44)

- Prepare for the possibility that there will be great division in your family.

    Do you think I came to bring peace on earth? No, I tell you, but division. From now on there will be five in one family divided against each other, three against

> two and two against three. They will be divided, father against son and son against father, mother against daughter and daughter against mother, mother-in-law against daughter-in-law and daughter-in-law against mother-in-law. (Luke 12:51–53)

- Burn all your bridges to the life you now live.

> Jesus replied, "No one who puts his hand to the plow and looks back is fit for service in the kingdom of God." (Luke 9:62)

- Be ready for the whole world to hate you.

> All men will hate you because of me, but he who stands firm to the end will be saved. (Mark 13:13)

- You could easily lose your job and reputation.

> They were stoned; they were sawed in two; they were put to death by the sword. They went about in sheepskins and goatskins, destitute, persecuted and mistreated—the world was not worthy of them. They wandered in deserts and mountains, and in caves and holes in the ground. (Hebrews 11:37–38)

- If you join a church truly of the Lord, you will be falsely accused of belonging to a cult.

> "We have found this man to be a troublemaker, stirring up riots among the Jews all over the world. He is a ringleader of the Nazarene sect . . ." (word "sect" is the same as cult). (Acts 24:5)

- Die having made yourself poor for others.

  > For you know the grace of our Lord Jesus Christ,
  > that though he was rich, yet for your sakes he be-
  > came poor, so that you through his poverty might
  > become rich. (2 Corinthians 8:9)

- A complete rejection of the ways of the world.

  > Do not conform any longer to the pattern of this
  > world, but be transformed by the renewing of your
  > mind. Then you will be able to test and approve what
  > God's will is—his good, pleasing and perfect will.
  > (Romans 12:2)

- A complete rejection of the things of the world.

  > Do not love the world or anything in the world. If
  > anyone loves the world, the love of the Father is not
  > in him. For everything in the world—the cravings
  > of sinful man, the lust of his eyes and the boasting
  > of what he has and does—comes not from the Fa-
  > ther but from the world. The world and its desires
  > pass away, but the man who does the will of God
  > lives forever. (1 John 2:15–17)

- A willingness to be persecuted for Jesus.

  > In fact, everyone who wants to live a godly life in
  > Christ Jesus will be persecuted, . . . (2 Timothy 3:12)

- A perseverance to suffer against sin until you are dead to sin.[46]

  > But the seed on good soil stands for those with a noble and good heart, who hear the word, retain it, and by persevering produce a crop. (Luke 8:15)

- A complete rejection of a good self-esteem.

  > I know that nothing good lives in me, that is, in my sinful nature. For I have the desire to do what is good, but I cannot carry it out. (Romans 7:18)

- A resolve to do God's will no matter what family, friends, wife, brothers, or sisters say about that will.

  > If anyone comes to me and does not hate his father and mother, his wife and children, his brothers and sisters—yes, even his own life—he cannot be my disciple. (Luke 14:26)

- A realization that God regretted making you.

  > The Lord was grieved that he had made man on the earth, and his heart was filled with pain. (Genesis 6:6)

- A sense of weakness, of being unable to live the Christian life.

  > That is why, for Christ's sake, I delight in weaknesses, in insults, in hardships, in persecutions, in difficulties. For when I am weak, then I am strong. (2 Corinthians 12:10)

50

- An absolute surrender and death to every aspect of self.

  > For the sinful nature desires what is contrary to the Spirit, and the Spirit what is contrary to the sinful nature. They are in conflict with each other, so that you do not do what you want. (Galatians 5:17)

- No attachment to anything in the world.

  > On that day no one who is on the roof of his house, with his goods inside, should go down to get them. Likewise, no one in the field should go back for anything. Remember Lot's wife! Whoever tries to keep his life will lose it, and whoever loses his life will preserve it. (Luke 17:31–33)

- To work out your salvation with fear and trembling, knowing you could lose it.[47]

  > Therefore, my dear friends, as you have always obeyed—not only in my presence, but now much more in my absence—continue to work out your salvation with fear and trembling. (Philippians 2:12)

- A resolve, if married, to live as though not married.

  > What I mean, brothers, is that the time is short. From now on those who have wives should live as if they had none. (1 Corinthians 7:29)

- To not look for a wife or husband if unmarried, but to wait on God.

    > Are you married? Do not seek a divorce. Are you unmarried? Do not look for a wife. (1 Corinthians 7:27)

- To pray all of the time.

    > . . . pray continually . . . (1 Thessalonians 5:17)

- To be devoted to church.

    > Be devoted to one another in brotherly love. Honor one another above yourselves. (Romans 12:10)

- Be prepared to stop associating with anyone who claims to be a Christian but is a hypocrite.

    > But now I am writing you that you must not associate with anyone who calls himself a brother but is sexually immoral or greedy, an idolater or a slanderer, a drunkard or a swindler. With such a man do not even eat. (1 Corinthians 5:11)

- Come into the Light where your whole life is open before God and the church.

    > But if we walk in the light, as he is in the light, we have fellowship with one another, and the blood of Jesus, his Son, purifies us from all sin. (1 John 1:7)

Are you willing for these things and more to be worked in your life by the power of God? Once a man or woman willingly strives to do only God's will, then comes the actual obedience by picking up the cross and following Jesus. Do you see why everyone must be a disciple? Just as Jesus carried His cross until He died on that cross, we cannot hope for a resurrected life without first carrying the cross the Holy Spirit gives us.[48] The apostles of Jesus gave up all and taught others the same.

Peter said to him, "We have left everything to follow you!" (Mark 10:28)

To "follow" Jesus requires that everyone leave "everything" behind. Only those who hate their lives surrender all. Only those who surrender will let the cross crucify them to the world.[49] And only those who allow themselves to be crucified unto death experience the resurrected life.

Truths to Ponder,
Beliefs to Examine

- Read back over the list in this chapter. Highlight or checkmark the things you see you need to do in your life.

- Ask God for the strength of His Spirit to be crucified with Christ.

CHAPTER 9

Why the Cross?

You should not be surprised at my saying, "You must be born again." (John 3:7)

We should not be "surprised" that we must be "born again." We are so totally worthless, vile, and corrupt that a brand new person must be created. Like the demons, we are completely undone, and we are like them in every way. The only difference between a demon and a man is that man has a choice. He can choose to be born again or refuse that chance. Demons had their chance in heaven and their opportunity has long passed. Hope does not exist in hell and there will be none for those who are not born again according to God's Word. As Paul declares, we are "worthless" and there is no one who "does good, not even one."

All have turned away, they have together become worthless; there is no one who does good, not even one. (Romans 3:12)

We must fully realize and be convinced by God, through the cross, who we really are.

- We are rebellious, turning away from God.
- We have become totally worthless.
- We are unable to do a single good thing.
- There is not even one person who honestly looks for God.

Apart from Jesus man does not have one good thing about him.[50] Apart from being born again not a single ounce of good dwells in a person. Paul goes on to declare the facts of who we are and the reason we must be born again.

> Their throats are open graves; their tongues practice deceit. The poison of vipers is on their lips. Their mouths are full of cursing and bitterness. Their feet are swift to shed blood; ruin and misery mark their ways, and the way of peace they do not know. There is no fear of God before their eyes. (Romans 3:13–18)

Look at your life and then look again at what Romans declares. Surely if you look honestly you will see that you are all these things and more:

- Throat is an open grave.
- Tongue practices deceit.
- The poison of vipers is on your lips.
- Mouth is full of cursing and bitterness.
- Feet are swift to shed blood.
- Ruin and misery mark your ways.

- The way of peace you do not know.
- There is no fear of God before your eyes.

Without conviction from the Holy Spirit and acceptance of these facts, a man never submits to God's way of salvation, for he always feels unjustly accused. God's grace requires full surrender of all pride and self-justification, for God is "grieved" that he made you. As He looks at your life and what you have become "pain" fills His heart.

> The Lord saw how great man's wickedness on the earth had become, and that every inclination of the thoughts of his heart was only evil all the time. The Lord was grieved that he had made man on the earth, and his heart was filled with pain. (Genesis 6:5–6)

As has been said, we are wicked to the core and God came to send all to hell who love being bad. God's only solution is to start over with you. A completely new you must be created. A new you conformed to Jesus' image, righteousness, and holiness. Jesus didn't die so you could clean up your life a bit.[51] God isn't going to patch you up to keep your life happy. God is not like a doctor or psychiatrist who seeks to hold you together, knowing full well it will soon all fall apart.

You remain beyond hope of ever doing anything good in your current state, so God must start over. That is what it means to be born again. A complete new life starts and grows into adulthood over time.[52] Growth requires a cross in your life that will slowly kill the old you, thus making room for the new you to grow.

The cross, however, must continue its work. When a man or woman stops carrying the cross, the new life God created starts to die because the old you begins to take over again. If this situation continues long enough, the new life God started totally dies and the person becomes more fit for hell than when God first started. Better that he never even started trying to be a Christian.[53]

Disciples carry their cross "daily"[54] and prepare themselves for death to self upon that cross. The "message of the cross" truly delivers a man from sin. As Paul declares, "it is the power of God" for those "being saved."

> For the message of the cross is foolishness to those who are perishing, but to us who are being saved it is the power of God. (1 Corinthians 1:18)

Those who wish to rely on a simple, cheap grace salvation message are not actually "being saved." Only those embracing the "message of the cross" are "being saved," for that is where the "power of God" dwells.

Truths to Ponder,
Beliefs to Examine

- What obstacles have you faced in the struggle to "be good enough?"

- How does it make you feel to read in Romans that you have become worthless?

- What areas in your life do you still feel have worth? Embrace the cross and allow Christ to crucify these things.

CHAPTER 10

The First Sermon

If someone decides to pay the cost, how then does he become a Christian? How does someone begin the process of being crucified to self? What does it really mean to believe in the Lord or to accept Jesus Christ as your personal Lord and Savior? Correct answers to these questions grant anyone a brand new life if he comes to God with faith. Answering correctly allows one to discover how to be "saved." For answers we need to look no further than the very first sermon Peter preached after Jesus' resurrection from the dead. All preachers and churches should imitate this model sermon if they want to present God's grace correctly.

"Therefore let all Israel be assured of this: God has made this Jesus, whom you crucified, both Lord and Christ." When the people heard this, they were cut to the heart and said to Peter and the other apostles, "Brothers, what shall we do?" Peter replied, "Repent and be baptized, every one of you, in the name of Jesus Christ for the forgiveness of your sins. And you will receive the gift of the

Holy Spirit. The promise is for you and your children and for all who are far off—for all whom the Lord our God will call." With many other words he warned them; and he pleaded with them, "Save yourselves from this corrupt generation." (Acts 2:36–40)

God shows that baptism is the next salvation step for those who have counted the cost. All the elements of Luke 14 are present in Peter's salvation sermon.

- The message of the cross is clearly presented. Because they knew Jesus' life,[55] they understood what the cross would mean for their lives.

  Therefore let all Israel be assured of this: God has made this Jesus, whom you crucified, both Lord and Christ. (verse 36)

- Deep conviction over their utter sinfulness came over them. They were "cut to the heart," about who they were before God. This was no intellectual understanding or selfish desire to be blessed by God. They knew they were enemies and the terms of peace was complete surrender of everything.

  . . . they were cut to the heart . . . (verse 37)

- They asked how to be saved and were broken and humble enough to accept God's way of righteousness. They did not argue or complain and look for some other way to ask Jesus into their life.

  "Brothers, what shall we do?" (verse 37)

All who "accepted" Peter's message, which was really God's offer of mercy, were baptized. Those who would not accept what Peter preached, forfeited eternal life in heaven.

> Those who accepted his message were baptized, and about three thousand were added to their number that day. (Acts 2:41)

They did not, as today, come forward and ask Jesus in their hearts, speak in tongues, or raise their hand and mock[56] back a prayer recited by the preacher. They were not so arrogant as to devise another way to salvation. Yet many will strive to discount the rest of Scripture by quoting Paul when he stated that God did not send him to baptize (1 Cor. 1:17). This is a staggering argument since Paul himself was baptized to "wash" "away" [his] "sins." Paul understood that God declared that the way a man washes away the sins in his life is through the cleansing waters of baptism. How can a man say his sins have been washed away, when he has not been washed?

> And now what are you waiting for [Paul]? Get up, be baptized and wash your sins away, calling on his name. (Acts 22:16)

In 1 Corinthians 1:17, Paul means that baptism is not to be used as some prideful act to gain followers. People quickly started saying, "I follow Paul" versus some other person.[57] It is natural for man's sinful nature to boast in whom they follow, and who wouldn't take some secret pride in being baptized by Paul? Jesus Himself did not baptize just for this reason, but He taught His disciples to baptize.[58] It wasn't that Paul did not baptize, he was just "thankful" he didn't in Corinth so that no one would fall into boasting. Indeed, Paul baptized Lydia and it was only after her baptism that she was able to "persuade[d]" them she was a "believer in the Lord."

> One of those listening was a woman named Lydia, a dealer in purple cloth from the city of Thyatira, who was a worshiper of God. The Lord opened her heart to respond to Paul's message. When she and the members of her household were baptized, she invited us to her home. "If you consider me a believer in the Lord," she said, "come and stay at my house." And she persuaded us. (Acts 16:14–15)

Notice that Paul baptized the jailer in Acts 16:33 and mature believers in Acts 19:5. Paul did not say that he never baptized. The point was that he personally did not baptize particular individuals because they might become puffed up in pride. To quote Paul, "I am thankful that I did not baptize any of you except Crispus and Gaius, *so no one can say that you were baptized into my name.*"[59] (emphasis added)

Paul and the apostles humbly submitted to God's righteous plan of saving man. They baptized in the name of the Father, Son, and Holy Spirit.[60] Preaching the complete and "full message"[61] caused everything to come together at once. They received the Holy Spirit, grace, mercy, and all the fullness of what it means to be saved all at one time. They did not complain that Peter made this salvation by works, therefore God could work His salvation in them.[62] Indeed, Peter later preached in the book of 1 Peter that "this water" saved them. To put it in his words, "this water symbolizes baptism that now saves you."

. . . and this water symbolizes baptism that now saves you also—not the removal of dirt from the body but the pledge of a good conscience toward God. It saves you by the resurrection of Jesus Christ, . . . (1 Peter 3:21)

Note well that water baptism receives its saving power from the "resurrection of Jesus Christ." Those who complain about it argue against Jesus being raised from the dead. In other words, the faith of Romans 10:10 comes alive for the first time through water baptism.[63] For only as we believe in our "heart and confess with our mouth that Jesus is Lord" will we have the kind of faith that can save us through water baptism.

Truths to Ponder,
Beliefs to Examine

- What elements of repentance were set in place in the believer's hearts in the book of Acts?

- Did anyone teach you about baptism? What were you told?

- How does that stand up to 1 Peter 3:21?

CHAPTER 11

The Full Message

But someone will say, "You have faith; I have deeds."
Show me your faith without deeds, and I will show you
my faith by what I do. (James 2:18)

Every Christian church and group requires certain "actions" that must be performed in order to receive salvation. Most groups say to just ask Jesus into your heart, others raise their hands, and some mock back a prayer. While some groups resort to a shallow application of water baptism, others mix it all up with speaking in tongues. Exactly what "action" does God have in mind for us to be saved? To put it in the words of the Scripture above, what does God require us to "do" in order to be saved? Let us look at the "full message" of God's good news.

"Go, stand in the temple courts," he said, "and tell the people the full message of this new life." (Acts 5:20)

Peter preached a "full message" of the "new life" in Jesus and was told to do so by an angel of the Lord. Everyone should stand in the "temple courts," fully out in the open preaching the "full message."

Teaching the "full message" of God's grace means that the "blood, water, and Spirit" are taught at the same time, for the three totally agree. No one aspect is more or less important than the other. The water cleanses the conscience, the blood signifies the cost of the cross, and the Spirit gives everything true faith and life. Correct preaching declares all three.

The book of Romans only declares a requirement of "baptism." It doesn't specify if that baptism is water, Spirit, or blood because it is all one baptism. The blood is just as important as the Spirit and the water is just as important as the blood and the Spirit.

> For there are three that testify: the Spirit, the water and the blood; and the three are in agreement. (1 John 5:7–8)

Individuals and churches that would not consider leaving the blood or Spirit of Jesus out of their gospel calls have no qualms about leaving out the water. Let this sin no longer continue. These three things, because God is Trinity in nature, testify to the unity of the message of the cross. When teaching is out of balance, God's people become hindered, walk in darkness, and are destroyed. In order to experience the resurrected life we must have all three aspects of Jesus. Why? First because no one can get to God "except through" Him. Second, "the way" of the cross in Jesus is God's method of salvation. And third, this is the only way to "the life" of abundance in God.

> Jesus answered, "I am the way and the truth and the life. No one comes to the Father except through me." (John 14:6)

Jesus comes to each of us and asks us to accept all of Him, to believe in every aspect of who He is and what He stands for. Jesus is Truth and those who love Christ worship all of Him. For this reason John states that Jesus "came by water and blood." John knew that all of Jesus was of equal importance and power. Truly the Spirit, blood, and water are all required for salvation. Every aspect of the Truth is necessary if we want to walk victorious in this world and arrive safely at heaven's gates.[64] The Holy Spirit "testifies" to this Truth.

> This is the one who came by water and blood—Jesus Christ. He did not come by water only, but by water and blood. And it is the Spirit who testifies, because the Spirit is the truth. (1 John 5:6)

In order for a man to be "born again," he must first see the need to be born again. He must utterly abhor himself and admit the need for the cross in his life. When a man sees this clearly and has counted the cost, he is ready to be born again through the waters of baptism by the power of the Holy Spirit and the blood of the Lamb. Jesus taught this lesson through Nicodemus, by teaching a man must be baptized in "water and Spirit" in order to be born again. Even natural birth demonstrates that the water and spirit are necessary. For there must be a spirit within a baby for there to be life, yet water surrounds the baby in the womb. Jesus uses the evidence of billions and billions of births to drive home the point that God's way of salvation comes through baptism.

As we will see in John 3:6, "flesh gives birth to flesh, but the Spirit gives birth to spirit." Both have their way of giving birth. Jesus teaches Nicodemus the way of the Spirit is through baptism. For "unless he is born of water and the Spirit" he cannot be born again. Nicodemus understood fully that Jesus was not talking about human birth, going back into the "womb," but about how to be born again by the power of the Holy Spirit.

> Now there was a man of the Pharisees named Nicodemus, a member of the Jewish ruling council. He came to Jesus at night and said, "Rabbi, we know you are a teacher who has come from God. For no one could perform the miraculous signs you are doing if God were not with him." In reply Jesus declared, "I tell you the truth, no one can see the kingdom of God unless he is born again." "How can a man be born when he is old?" Nicodemus asked. "Surely he cannot enter a second time into his mother's womb to be born!" Jesus answered, "I tell you the truth, no one can enter the kingdom of God unless he is born of water and the Spirit. Flesh gives birth to flesh, but the Spirit gives birth to spirit. You should not be surprised at my saying, 'You must be born again.'" (John 3:1–7)

Man cannot be born again by saying a prayer, speaking in tongues, attending classes, or any other works man might devise. After all, is baptism more "works" than a prayer?

Of course not; being baptized or saying a prayer to be saved both involve "doing" something. Therefore, doing something is a moot point. The only question is what did God command us to do in order to be saved? God did not tell us to speak a prayer to gain salvation. He declared that a man must be "born of water and the Spirit" in order to be born again. Among many, in an effort to make easy the grace of God, they have forgotten that Jesus also "came by water" as well as by "blood."

> This is the one who came by water and blood—Jesus Christ. He did not come by water only, but by water and blood. And it is the Spirit who testifies, because the Spirit is the truth. (1 John 5:6)

Truths to Ponder,
Beliefs to Examine

- In what ways does the description of baptism in this chapter surprise you?

- What parts of the "full message" were you never taught?

- Meditate on the truth of 1 John 5:6. Have you been truly born again?

CHAPTER 12

Giving Orders

God demands that action and faith work together. Indeed, faith without action is not faith at all in God's sight. The book of James drives home the point by asking the following question:

> You foolish man, do you want evidence that faith without deeds is useless? (James 2:20)

This isn't earning salvation, rather it allows the salvation power of God to work and will in us.[65] Many stop the grace of God from producing works in them because of their stubborn hearts or bad teaching. For them, grace is without effect.[66]

While this publication cannot possibly refute every objection that stubborn hearts pose, let us at least answer the question of the thief on the cross. Some question if baptism of water, blood, and Spirit are required for salvation how could the thief on the cross go to heaven?[67] Look at the heart of God for the answer.[68]

Obviously if one cannot find water, or circumstances prevent baptism, they will be saved.[69] God sees the heart and knows His children.[70] However, if people's hearts truly love God, they gladly obey all of God's commands for the reasons God declares, as soon as the opportunity presents itself.[71] Consider well, that if Jesus did not exempt Himself from baptism, even though He did not need to be baptized, under what justification do you excuse yourself?[72]

Know this; even if you think you have the Holy Spirit, you still must be water baptized for salvation. Indeed, you are "ordered" to be water baptized for the reasons God states.

> "Can anyone keep these people from being baptized with water? They have received the Holy Spirit just as we have." So he *ordered* that they be baptized in the name of Jesus Christ. Then they asked Peter to stay with them for a few days. (Acts 10:47–48 emphasis added)

As we look deeper at the meaning of water baptism, we can destroy another excuse or question, "What if I were in the desert? What then?" Of course God works and wills to provide in every situation.[73] For if God is powerful enough to give us a way out when tempted,[74] He can certainly make a way for us to be righteous. Just look at the following true incident. Let us follow Philip on the "desert road" and see what happened. Note well it was a "desert road," a place where one could go miles without even a hint of water to drink, let alone enough to be immersed or baptized.[75]

Now an angel of the Lord said to Philip, "Go south to the road—the desert road—that goes down from Jerusalem to Gaza." (Acts 8:26)

The Ethiopian eunuch's story begins by studying the book of Isaiah and ends with water baptism. Philip begins "with that very passage of Scripture" and concludes with water baptism. So it should be with us. As we talk about the Holy Spirit, grace, mercy, or any other passage of Scripture with an unbeliever, we should end with water baptism. If we preach the true "good news about Jesus" we will end where Philip ended, standing in water.

Then Philip began with that very passage of Scripture and told him the good news about Jesus. As they traveled along the road, they came to some water and the eunuch said, "Look, here is water. Why shouldn't I be baptized?" And he gave orders to stop the chariot. Then both Philip and the eunuch went down into the water and Philip baptized him. When they came up out of the water, the Spirit of the Lord suddenly took Philip away, and the eunuch did not see him again, but went on his way rejoicing. Philip, however, appeared at Azotus and traveled about, preaching the gospel in all the towns until he reached Caesarea. (Act 8:35–40)

"Look, here is water," the eunuch exclaimed. Somehow, from the preaching of Philip, the eunuch came to a correct conclusion about how to be saved. In his determination the eunuch gave "orders" for the chariot to stop so he could be water baptized. The God who controls the universe and arranges where men should live[76] knew that this exact moment required water. Even in a desert, God can work and will His full message of salvation if the heart willingly responds to God's grace.[77] With tender hearts "both Philip and the eunuch went down into the water" to baptize the eunuch. Coming "up out of the water," they each went the way of God's will as disciples of Jesus.

Truths to Ponder,
Beliefs to Examine

- What questions or arguments arise in your mind about baptism?

- How does the story of the Ethiopian eunuch answer these doubts?

- Why did the Eunuch go on his way rejoicing? Does this knowledge of baptism cause you to rejoice? Why or why not?

CHAPTER 13

A Daily Cross

The cross kills the very essence of who you are and destroys your very self and life, while God creates a totally new you. When this happens, God gives you a new self, made in the image of Jesus to replace the one crucified unto death. Water baptism begins the process. God plants the seed of new life in you at baptism. And as the old dies, the new comes to life each day.[78] The same book in the Bible that speaks of confessing with our mouths and believing in our hearts, tells us how to be "freed from sin." Paul tells us baptism is the key.

> What shall we say, then? Shall we go on sinning so that grace may increase? By no means! We died to sin; how can we live in it any longer? Or don't you know that all of us who were baptized into Christ Jesus were baptized into his death? We were therefore buried with him through baptism into death in order that, just as Christ was raised from the dead through the glory of

the Father, we too may live a new life. If we have been united with him like this in his death, we will certainly also be united with him in his resurrection. For we know that our old self was crucified with him so that the body of sin might be done away with, that we should no longer be slaves to sin—because anyone who has died has been freed from sin. (Romans 6:1–7)

A man dies to sin by being "buried" with Christ "into death" so that God can give him a "new life." Apart from this call to baptism, little of the true resurrected life exists. For no man can "know that" his "old self was crucified" if he has not been "united with him *like this* in his death" (emphasis added). This is one reason why infant baptism is completely rejected. There is no way for babies to understand what happens to them, nor have an opportunity to count the cost to recognize themselves as sinners[79] and obtain faith from God.[80]

Going under the water symbolizes entering the tomb with Jesus and dying to ourselves. Coming "up" out of the water represents a resurrected person in the image of Jesus, just as Jesus was resurrected up out of the tomb.

A man can ask Jesus into his heart all day long, but without this baptism the "old self" has not been crucified and put to death. Would you like to no longer be a slave to sin? Then submit to God's righteousness instead of trying to establish and live by your church's doctrine or personal opinion.

During water baptism, a man or woman picks up the cross that comes from Jesus for the very first time. Men and women in churches throughout the world pick up crosses to carry, but that does not mean Jesus chose those crosses for them.[81] This is why Jesus ended with saying, "and follow me." Without following Jesus the cross they carry has no power to save, deliver, or change them. A man must pick up a daily cross if he expects the salvation of God in his life. In order for the saving grace to enter a man's soul, there must spring to life deep denial of self that has the cross as its central focus unto a resurrected life.[82]

> Then he said to them all: "If anyone would come after me, he must deny himself and take up his cross daily and follow me." (Luke 9:23)

It is the daily cross that causes us to mature in Jesus. Without this daily crucifixion the new self withers and slowly dies.[83] So slow that the person doesn't even notice they are falling away.[84] For this reason, Peter urged us to make sure we grow up in our faith. If we refuse to "make" our "calling and election sure" then we will "fall."

> Therefore, my brothers, be all the more eager to make your calling and election sure. For if you do these things, you will never fall, and you will receive a rich welcome into the eternal kingdom of our Lord and Savior Jesus Christ. (2 Peter 1:10–11)

Like babies, Peter urges new believers to "crave pure spiritual milk."[85] Carrying a daily cross allows the Word of God to mature us and to make us strong. Those who "daily" are crucified to a little bit more self "will receive a rich welcome into the eternal kingdom" of Jesus.

Truths to Ponder, Beliefs to Examine

- How can someone die daily?

- What sins in your life do you need to bury with Christ?

- Describe the cross Christ has in your life.

CHAPTER 14

Having This Attitude

The new life begins, but God desires for us to go on to maturity.[86] Indeed, only those who produce a good crop in maturity will be found worthy of eternal life.[87] Just as every good parent desires for their child to grow up and display good qualities, so too God desires the same in our lives.[88] For this reason, we need to carry our cross daily to grow.[89] The question begs itself, are you willing to carry your cross daily and suffer against sin in order to overcome?[90] For God's Word tells us only those who "overcome"[91] reside in heaven with Jesus. Listen to the preaching of Peter again about the cross in a disciple's life.

> Therefore, since Christ suffered in his body, arm yourselves also with the same attitude, because he who has suffered in his body is done with sin. As a result, he does not live the rest of his earthly life for evil human desires, but rather for the will of God. (1 Peter 4:1–2)

When Jesus was crucified on the cross, He felt the pain of nails in His hands and feet. He agonized as death came by inches and slowly over hours. Indeed, He suffered humiliation as they whipped, beat, and terrorized Him before making Him carry the cross outside Jerusalem. Dying on the cross became a very real physical matter for Jesus. It was no intellectual religious mind exercise, but rather suffering death combined with spiritual turmoil and battle. Peter encourages us to obtain this "same attitude," because only those who have "suffered" in their bodies are "done with sin." Only those who "suffer," feeling in their bodies in a very physical way the power of the cross, can walk the new life in Jesus.

The resurrected life happens only as a "result" of suffering by the power of the cross with sin. Very few churches have experienced this cleansing power from blood shed on a cross. Fellowship in the Light in a church that understands the power of suffering with Jesus causes the "blood of Jesus" to purify "us from all sin."

> But if we walk in the light, as he is in the light, we have fellowship with one another, and the blood of Jesus, his Son, purifies us from all sin. (1 John 1:7)

A person can only do God's will by suffering against sin because the flesh must be dealt with first. Most just do not want that kind of saving grace and turn to the multitude of self-help books, deliverance ministries, support groups, and revival meetings that dot the land. It is much easier to talk about sin than to suffer in one's body. It is simpler to pray with everyone about problems than to suffer and die on the cross over them. As a result, the church embraces many other ways to deal with sin other than the cross. Few want to suffer enough on the cross against sin to be dead to it. Most remain selfishly content and lazy to just let Jesus do all the suffering for them. They do not love Him enough to suffer with Him.

To preach or live anything less than this message is to live a lie. If we desire to experience the life-changing power of God every day, we must also share equally in the suffering of the cross. As Paul joyously declares, "we always carry around in our body the death of Jesus, so that the life of Jesus" may be in us. If you are willing to "always" have the death of Jesus working in you then you can expect His powerful life to also reside in you.

> We always carry around in our body the death of Jesus,
> so that the life of Jesus may also be revealed in our body.
> (2 Corinthians 4:10)

The true Holy Spirit-inspired Christian walk shares in the sufferings of Jesus. In other words, no one really enjoys the comforts of Jesus if we do not have his sufferings flowing into our lives. The vast majority of church goers experience the false salvation, one without the sufferings of Christ. They have a comfort, but it will only last in this world. A disciple's "comfort overflows" in his life because the "sufferings of Christ" also fill his life.

> For just as the sufferings of Christ flow over into our
> lives, so also through Christ our comfort overflows.
> (2 Corinthians 1:5)

Any preaching or life lived differently than this supports false Christianity. Only those who "share in the sufferings" of Christ on an hourly basis can claim the title of true "children" of God. No one is an "heir" of the good things to come unless they "indeed" suffer in their bodies with and against sin.

> Now if we are children, then we are heirs—heirs of God and co-heirs with Christ, if indeed we share in his sufferings in order that we may also share in his glory. (Romans 8:17)

If you desire the "glory" of God that overcomes sin, then you must share in the sufferings of Christ. If you are willing to pay the price, then begin today by being crucified to yourself and God will give you the beginnings of a new life.

Quick fixes for our sin do not exist. No wide gate or road leads to salvation. Instead, we must enter through a narrow gate and walk a narrow road to heaven. Jesus said only a "few find it" while "many" enter through the wide gate of just asking Jesus in their heart, to their destruction.

> Enter through the narrow gate. For wide is the gate and broad is the road that leads to destruction, and many enter through it. But small is the gate and narrow the road that leads to life, and only a few find it. (Matthew 7:13–14)

Again, are you willing to pay the cost for such a life of discipleship? Do you really hate sin and wickedness enough to give it all up so that God's righteousness may remain in you? If so, plant this attitude in your heart and mind by the power of the Holy Spirit. Many do not really want the power to overcome sin. They love the flesh and sinfulness too much. They have no real desire to be made well and would rather spend their time making excuses as to why they have not changed.[92] God will give you the power to live all of this, it is simply a matter of whether you really want to be a disciple.[93]

Truths to Ponder,
Beliefs to Examine

• Describe Jesus' attitude in suffering on the cross.

• Explain how you can have the same attitude.

• What steps can you take to enter the narrow gate?

CHAPTER 15

Why Become a Christian?

This is the verdict: Light has come into the world, but men loved darkness instead of light because their deeds were evil. Everyone who does evil hates the light, and will not come into the light for fear that his deeds will be exposed. (John 3:19–20)

Whether you honestly want God's mercy and grace can be answered with a very simple question. Are you tired of a life in the darkness and do you hunger for light? Jesus died for mankind to allow those who hunger for holiness, truth, goodness, purity, and love a chance to possess these qualities.[94] Those who hate evil come into the light to become righteous like Jesus.[95] In short, there is only one real reason why someone would want to become a disciple.

You might be asking yourself, with all the suffering and loss involved in a Christian's life why would anyone want to be a disciple? The answer is very simple, yet few want it.

It is a matter of loving God. True love for God is stronger than death, even death to self.[96] God is holy, perfect love[97] and those who desire God want to be with Him, and be like their Father.

Which Father do you want to be like? Those who do not love God this way belong to their "father, the devil" and want to do what pleases him and themselves. There is no middle ground, either it is the cross in a man's life or it is the devil in his life.

> You belong to your father, the devil, and you want to carry out your father's desire . . . (John 8:44)

Disciples love what is good, and God is very good. In fact, God is the only one good and in loving Him we love all that is good.[98] Only when we desire everything "noble, right, pure, lovely, admirable, excellent, and praiseworthy" can we expect the "God of peace" in our lives. God only loves and fellowships with those who love righteousness.[99] Those who come to Jesus just because their lives are miserable are in for a terrible shock on judgment day.[100]

> Finally, brothers, whatever is true, whatever is noble, whatever is right, whatever is pure, whatever is lovely, whatever is admirable—if anything is excellent or praise-worthy—think about such things. Whatever you have learned or received or heard from me, or seen in me—put it into practice. And the God of peace will be with you. (Philippians 4:8–9)

Now is our time of "testing."[101] A man who loves God, loves righteousness, truth, and holiness no matter the suffering or loss.[102] Those who love wickedness want a false Jesus who will bless them in a worldly manner.[103] If you love God with a true desire, you consider the cross in your life a thing of beauty and joy. The cross forms a person into the image of Jesus and is God's method for making us ready for His holiness. Those dying to themselves are transformed into the likeness of Jesus and therefore sin gradually vanishes. A true Christian sins less and less each day. If you know someone who claims to be a Christian but is a hypocrite,[104] they are not really of Jesus. Because Jesus "appeared" to "take away our sins" so that a person will stop sinning."

> But you know that he appeared so that he might take away our sins. And in him is no sin. No one who lives in him keeps on sinning. No one who continues to sin has either seen him or known him. (1 John 3:5–6)

Anyone who tells you they know God but continues to sin is a liar. Just like the demons who believe in God but keep on sinning, so too, such people have a demonic faith without the life-changing power of a crucifying cross. Don't "let anyone lead you astray" in this matter. Someone who honestly follows Jesus will stop sinning. A true disciple sees new sins to die to each day while they stop the old sins of the past from rising up. Indeed, they "cannot go on sinning, because" they have "been born of God."

> Dear children, do not let anyone lead you astray. He who does what is right is righteous, just as he is righteous. He who does what is sinful is of the devil, because the devil has been sinning from the beginning. The reason the Son of God appeared was to destroy the devil's work.

> No one who is born of God will continue to sin, because God's seed remains in him; he cannot go on sinning, because he has been born of God. (1 John 3:7–9)

If you do not find the cross to be a joy, the odds are you will persecute those who do follow Jesus on the narrow road.[105] Think about Moses who made a conscious choice to be "mistreated" with the "people of God rather than to enjoy the pleasures of sin for a short time." Admittedly, sin is fun and enjoyable, while the cross brings pain and crucifies us to the world. If someone portrays Christianity as fun and enjoyable, they preach a false Jesus.[106]

> He chose to be mistreated along with the people of God rather than to enjoy the pleasures of sin for a short time. He regarded disgrace for the sake of Christ as of greater value than the treasures of Egypt, because he was looking ahead to his reward. (Hebrews 11:25–26)

The cross gives us each a choice. If we "value" the "treasures of Egypt"[107] more than the love of God, we reject this message. Our acceptance or rejection of the message of the cross reveals who and what we love.

If you "hunger and thirst for righteousness," God makes you into a brand new person so that your righteousness results from His power.

> Blessed are those who hunger and thirst for righteousness, for they will be filled. (Matthew 5:6)

The salvation call of Jesus comes with true "authority" and power.[108] His salvation call demands we obey all He requires by the power of the Holy Spirit through faith.[109] This is what God means by "grace," it is His power in us to say "No" to sin.[110] The good news of God grants us a "festival" of righteousness, denying self, and hating our lives in this world.[111] The good news lets us obey God, having our sins washed away, so that we can enjoy sweet fellowship with Him.[112] God's amazing grace gives us the power to become totally new creations.[113] Those who merely want the blessings of God apart from the crucified life use God to indulge themselves in their sinful desires. They are like demons who believe in God, yet are still demons by nature. Like devils, they want the things of God for their own ends, but are not in love with God's character. Those who honestly love God want to be like Jesus, and Jesus became who He was, as the Son of Man, by the cross manifested in His life. A true disciple lives for the hope of being "like him." If we really love Jesus then we will want to imitate him while we are in "this world." Only with this message can we have "confidence" that our faith is ready for "the day of judgment."

> In this way, love is made complete among us so that we will have confidence on the day of judgment, because in this world we are like him. (1 John 4:17)

Truths to Ponder,
Beliefs to Examine

- Define a true disciple of Christ.

- Did you ever think it possible to stop sinning?

- List some "little" sins in your life that you thought would never stop.

- Determine to place them at the cross one at a time.

CHAPTER 16

The First Step of Humility

Then Philip ran up to the chariot and heard the man reading Isaiah the prophet. "Do you understand what you are
reading?" Philip asked. "How can I," he said, "unless
someone explains it to me?" So he invited Philip to come
up and sit with him. (Acts 8:30–31)

Do you understand what you are reading?" Be humble
enough like the eunuch in the story above to say, "How
can I?" The cross crucifies pride. Like the eunuch, find a
true disciple of Jesus to "invite[d]" into your life who can
teach you to count the cost and baptize you "in the name of
the Father, Son, and Holy Spirit." God will honor this, and
you will begin a new day, with a new life as a disciple of
Jesus. Ask God to send you someone who understands what
it means to count the cost, how to suffer against sin, how
to count suffering as a joy, who denies self unto death, and
knows how to really be born again. Find someone without
a legalistic or shallow understanding of water baptism, but

who themselves have walked through the narrow gate by the power of the Holy Spirit.[114]

Usually a person will think this is beyond them to live. They feel hopeless in attempting to live this kind of Christianity. Many voiced this very concern to Jesus and He simply told them to make "every effort."[115] The good news is that if you want to love God, He will give you His power to walk the narrow road.

The message of the cross is not a matter of a bunch of rules, principles, and applications of dos or don'ts. Rather it means surrendering to God to do the work through you.[116] So the question isn't whether you can live this kind of life, it is a question of whether you are willing to let Jesus honestly be Lord of your life. Only those who say it is "hopeless" to live this life will be given divine power to walk the narrow road.[117]

Pray for God to show you who preaches and lives the "full message." Many groups preach only the Spirit, (blessings, miracles, feelings) and therefore remove the blood (cost, suffering, testimonies) and these partial gospels can never deliver one from sin. Many others speak of only the blood, (cost, denying self) but do not have the Spirit (oil, joy) or the water (refreshment, purity) all of which leaves the believer despondent and weak. Still other groups preach the water of Jesus but forget the blood and the Spirit. For them Jesus is an intellectual or feel-good experience. Let God lead you to a church where you feel uncomfortable. After all, the cross is not a comfortable thing to hang on and a church preaching the complete message of the cross can feel very unsettling to join.[118] If you can't find someone with these basics down, realize that they offer you, at best, only part of the good news. After all, if the foundation is faulty there is a greater danger the house will collapse.[119]

The salvation call of Jesus includes the altar of sacrifice that will forever change a man. The old Law of the Bible required many sacrifices burnt on the altar for sins. Jesus completed the law by offering Himself as a sacrifice for our sins. Jesus lived a life continually sacrificing Himself to God. And those born again, in the image of Jesus, live a life of continual sacrifice to God. Disciples of Jesus walk in the footsteps of Jesus by daily offering their "bodies" as living sacrifices.

> Therefore, I urge you, brothers, in view of God's mercy, to offer your bodies as living sacrifices, holy and pleasing to God—this is your spiritual act of worship. (Romans 12:1)

A true "act of worship" towards God requires that a man or woman sacrifice themselves to God. God's "mercy" motivates a thankful-hearted[120] person to become a disciple.[121] Without sacrificing everything to God, we have no hope of salvation.[122] Are you ready, with joy in your heart, to count the cost, pay the price, and become a disciple? If so the Scripture below is for you. If you desire to "obey everything" by the new self that God will create, then Jesus commands you to become a "disciple," by being baptized in the name of the "Father, Son, and Holy Spirit." Then every day, as you grow in the Lord, confess with your mouth and believe in your heart that Jesus is Lord. Then your faith will be real and it will provide the blessing of saving your soul.

> Then Jesus came to them and said, "All authority in heaven and on earth has been given to me. Therefore go and make disciples of all nations, baptizing them in the name of the Father and of the Son and of the Holy Spirit, and teaching them to obey everything I have commanded you. And surely I am with you always, to the very end of the age." (Matthew 28:18–20)

What a blessing it is to know Jesus remains "always" with us "to the very end of the age." Those who obey God by faith have the right and the privilege to walk in this blessing.[123] As we have seen, God only gives the Holy Spirit to those who "obey him." Those who have true faith in God obey Him in this way, by the power of the Holy Spirit and for the reasons He commands. Faith gives the power to obey and the new life springs from obedience to God. Note well that God only gives the Holy Spirit to those who "obey him" day in and day out.

> We are witnesses of these things, and so is the Holy Spirit, whom God has given to those who *obey him*." (Acts 5:32 emphasis added)

It happens all by faith, but the new life is maintained and grows only as we obey the Holy Spirit with a living faith.[124] For a man who says he believes something but does not act with the power of that belief is as a demon. After all, "even the demons believe—and shudder."

EVERYTHING SAID

With everything said, look to God whose ways can save you from cheap grace and never-ending death in hell.

For you have delivered me from death and my feet from stumbling, that I may walk before God in the light of life. (Psalm 56:13)

ENDNOTES

1. 1 Corinthians 1:12–13
2. Ephesians 6:24
3. Isaiah 26:10
4. 1 Corinthians 2:4
5. Luke 14:25–35 Large crowds were traveling with Jesus, and turning to them he said: "If anyone comes to me and does not hate his father and mother, his wife and children, his brothers and sisters—yes, even his own life—he cannot be my disciple. And anyone who does not carry his cross and follow me cannot be my disciple. Suppose one of you wants to build a tower. Will he not first sit down and estimate the cost to see if he has enough money to complete it? For if he lays the foundation and is not able to finish it, everyone who sees it will ridicule him, saying, 'This fellow began to build and was not able to finish.' Or suppose a king is about to go to war against another king. Will he not first sit down and consider whether he is able with ten thousand men to oppose the one coming against him with twenty thousand? If he is not able, he will send a delegation while the other is still a long way off and will ask for terms of peace. In the same way, any of you who does not give up everything he has cannot be my disciple. Salt is good, but if it loses its saltiness, how can it be made salty again? It is fit neither for the soil nor

for the manure pile; it is thrown out. He who has ears to hear, let him hear."

6. Psalm 49:13

7. Ecclesiastes 3:11

8. Mark 1:24

9. Hebrews 10:31

10. 2 Corinthians 13:5

11. Genesis 3:1

12. Galatians 5:6

13. Matthew 22:12

14. Galatians 4:19

15. Mark 10:21, Luke 9:59–62

16. Acts 14:22, note "many hardships."

17. John 16:33

18. 1 John 2:6

19. 1 Corinthians 13:12

20. Mark 4:17, Hebrews 6:6

21. Acts 11:26, literally "little Christ."

22. Acts 6:1, 6:7, 9:1, 9:19, 9:26, 18:23, 18:27, 19:1, 21:4–5

23. Disciples are individuals that were saved, are being saved and will be saved. Salvation, like discipleship, is a process. God has given us free choice and we can stop this process of saving grace and thus fall away, (Hebrews 6:4–8). Romans 10:10, 2 Corinthians 2:15, 1 Peter 1:5, 1 Corinthians 1:18, Ephesians 2:5, Philippians 1:28, 2 Timothy 1:9, Hebrews 9:28, 1 Thessalonians 5:8, Romans 8:24, Ephesians 1:13–14, Romans 13:11, Ephesians 1:4–5.

24. Hebrews 6:7

25. Hebrews 6:7–8

26. Hebrews 3:15

27. Jude 1:24

28. John 15:6

29. Lamentations 3:28

30. John 4:14

31. Isaiah 48:22

32. Revelation 6:12–17
33. Ezekiel 13:10–15
34. Revelation 14:11
35. 2 Peter 3:14
36. Matthew 7:22
37. Psalm 50:5
38. Philippians 3:19
39. Luke 17:33
40. Matthew 7:13
41. 2 Timothy 4:7
42. Matthew 22:12
43. Matthew 25:31–46
44. 1 John 4:16
45. *The Essential Piece, Living Out Luke 14:26 in Everyday Life*, Timothy Williams (Enumclaw, WA: WinePress Publishing, 2000), ISBN 1-57921-293-X, or *A Whisper Revival—Our Only Option*, Timothy Williams (Enumclaw, WA: WinePress Publishing, 2000)
46. 1 Peter 4:1–2
47. Hebrews 6:6
48. Romans 8:13
49. Galatians 6:14
50. Proverbs 12:10, note: the "kindest acts of the wicked are cruel."
51. Matthew 12:43–44
52. 1 Peter 2:2
53. 2 Peter 2:21–22
54. Luke 9:23
55. John 12:32, Galatians 3:1
56. Proverbs 1:22
57. 1 Corinthians 1:12, 3:4
58. John 4:2, 1 Corinthians 1:12
59. 1 Corinthians 1:14–15 (emphasis added)
60. Matthew 28:19
61. Acts 5:20

62. John 6:65

63. Romans 10:10

64. Hosea 4:6

65. Acts 26:19, 1 Corinthians 15:10

66. 1 Corinthians 15:10

67. Luke 23:43 Jesus answered him, "I tell you the truth, today you will be with me in paradise."

68. Mark 2:27, note: For example, the Law demanded a Sabbath rest, but the law would be misunderstood if the heart of God was not taken into account.

69. Romans 2:25–29

70. 2 Timothy 2:19

71. Ephesians 5:15–16

72. Matthew 3:15

73. 1 Corinthians 10:13

74. 1 Corinthians 10:13

75. The word baptism means immersed.

76. Acts 17:26

77. Ephesians 1:11

78. 2 Corinthians 5:17

79. Psalm 51:5

80. John 6:44

81. John 21:22

82. Many will "heap abuse" on you for your life of denying self. Do not let them stop you from following Jesus. 1 Peter 4:4

83. John 15:6

84. Revelation 3:1–2

85. 1 Peter 2:2

86. Hebrews 6:1, Hebrews 5:12

87. Luke 8:14–15

88. Hebrews 12:10

89. Luke 8:14

90. Hebrews 12:4

91. 1 John 5:5, Revelation 2:7, 2:11, 2:17, 2:26, 3:5, 3:12, 3:21, 21:7
92. Ezekiel 18:2–3, John 5:6
93. John 15:4–5
94. Matthew 5:6
95. John 3:20–21
96. Song of Songs 8:6
97. 1 John 4:16
98. Mark 10:18
99. Daniel 9:4
100. Luke 17:17
101. Hebrews 3:8
102. Revelation 22:11–12
103. Psalm 17:14
104. 1 Corinthians 5:11
105. 2 Timothy 3:12
106. Galatians 6:14, 1 John 2:15, 2 Timothy 3:4, Micah 2:11
107. Egypt in the Bible symbolizes the world with all of its goods and pleasures.
108. Matthew 7:29
109. Matthew 28:20
110. Titus 2:12
111. 1 Corinthians 5:8
112. 1 Peter 3:21
113. Titus 2:12
114. Matthew 7:13
115. Luke 13:23–24
116. Colossians 2:23
117. Isaiah 57:10
118. Acts 5:13
119. 1 Corinthians 3:10–14
120. 1 John 4:19
121. 1 John 4:19

122. Hebrews 9:22
123. Psalm 50:16
124. Romans 1:17

To order additional copies of

Call

Toll free: (877) 421-READ (7323)

or send $7.95** each, plus $4.45* S&H to

WinePress Publishing
PO Box 428
Enumclaw, WA 98022

www.winepresspub.com

or

For special discount ministry and group prices contact:

Sound Doctrine
PO Box 856
Enumclaw, WA 98022 USA
(360) 802-2550

**WA residents, add 8.4% sales tax

*add $1.00 S&H for each additional
book ordered

For more information about
becoming a disciple contact:

SOUND DOCTRINE
P.O. Box 856
Enumclaw, WA 98022
(360) 802-2550
www.sdoctrine.org